P9-CNB-871

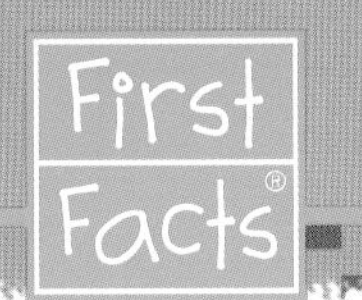

ELITE MILITARY FORCES

THE DELTA FORCE

by Jennifer M. Besel

CAPSTONE PRESS
a capstone imprint

First Facts is published by Capstone Press,
151 Good Counsel Drive, P.O. Box 669, Mankato, Minnesota 56002.
www.capstonepub.com

Books published by Capstone Press are manufactured with paper containing at least 10 percent post-consumer waste.

Library of Congress Cataloging-in-Publication Data
Besel, Jennifer M.
The Delta Force / by Jennifer M. Besel.
p. cm.—(First facts. Elite military forces)
Summary: "Provides information on the U.S. Delta Force, including their training, missions, and equipment"—Provided by publisher.
Includes bibliographical references and index.
ISBN 978-1-4296-5382-4 (library binding)
1. United States. Army. Delta Force—Juvenile literature. I. Title. II. Series.
UA34.S64B468 2011
356'.16—dc22 2010029385

Editorial credits:
Christine Peterson, editor; Matt Bruning, designer; Laura Manthe, production specialist

Photo credits:
Getty Images Inc./AFP/Shah Marai, 19; The Image Bank/MILpictures by Tom Weber, 21; iStockphoto/Roberto A Sanchez, cover; Photo by Spc. Tony Hawkins, USASOC PAO, 5; Shutterstock/Jaroslaw Grudzinski, 17 (pistol); tatniz, 17 (vest); Triff, 5; U.S. Army photo by SFC; Silas Toney, 7; Staff Sgt. Drew Lockwood, 11; USASOC News Service, 8, 13, 14; Wikimedia/Dybdal, 17 (rifle)

Artistic Effects
iStockphoto/Brett Charlton, Craig DeBourbon; Shutterstock/koh sze kiat, Maksym Bondarchuk, Masonjar, Péter Gudella, reventon2527, Serg64, Tom Grundy

Printed in the United States of America in Melrose Park, Illinois.
092010 005935LKS11

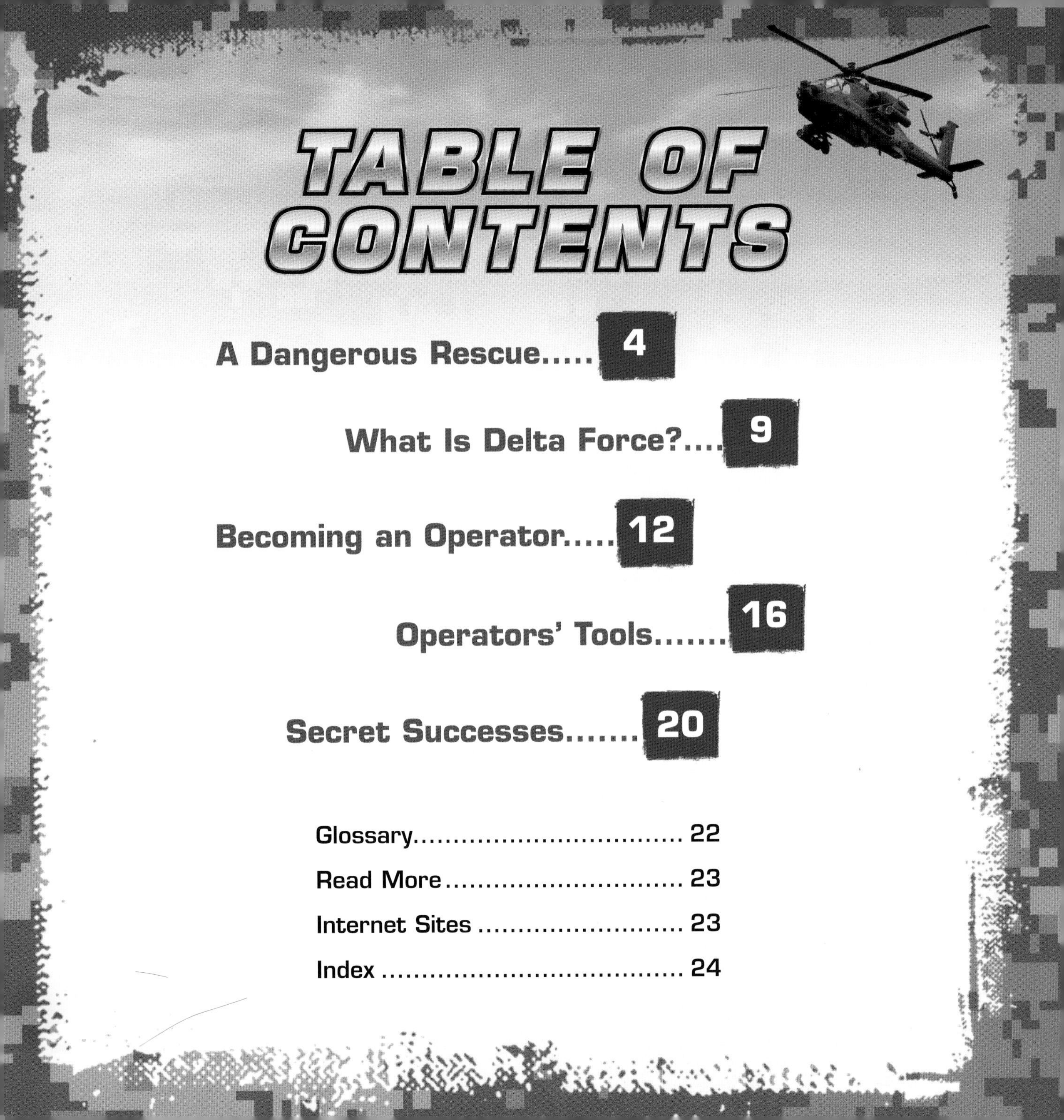

TABLE OF CONTENTS

A DANGEROUS RESCUE

Four MH-6 helicopters soar through the night sky. Onboard, 23 Delta Force **operators** prepare for a rescue mission. Enemies are holding a U.S. citizen **hostage** in a prison. The operators' job is to free him. The helicopters land on the roof. Wearing night-vision goggles, operators storm the prison.

operator: a soldier who is a member of Delta Force

hostage: a person held prisoner by an enemy

The Delta Force operators break into teams. Some search for the enemy. As bullets fly down the prison halls, another team finds the hostage. They shoot the lock off his prison cell. With the hostage freed, the teams leave quickly. They leap into the helicopters and disappear into the night.

The full name of the team is First Special Forces Operational Detachment-Delta. But team members just call it the Unit.

WHAT IS DELTA FORCE?

Delta Force is the U.S. military's most secret team of soldiers. Delta Force operators go on dangerous missions around the world. Their goal is to stop **terrorists**. They work undercover to keep the United States safe.

terrorist: someone who uses violence to achieve a goal

Delta Force operators do whatever it takes to stop terrorists. To spy on enemies, they dress and speak like people from other countries. They climb mountains to destroy enemy weapons. Operators work day and night to complete their missions.

Current U.S. military rules allow only men to serve in Delta Force.

BECOMING AN OPERATOR

Only the best soldiers may try out for Delta Force. Unit leaders look for men who speak different languages. They also want soldiers with strong computer skills.

During **selection**, the men run day and night. In the final test, they cross 40 miles (64 kilometers) of mountains. Carrying a heavy pack and a rifle, each man must finish in less than a day.

selection: the testing period to be picked for Delta Force

Few soldiers pass the four-week selection test.

FACT

Each operator shoots 50,000 bullets a year just in training exercises.

Men who pass selection become operators. Operators train for six months. Experts teach them how to use explosives to blow open doors. They learn to rescue people from **hijacked** airplanes. **CIA** agents show them how to get secret information. They learn to shoot with accuracy.

hijack: to take illegal control of a vehicle

CIA: a U.S. government spy organization

OPERATORS' TOOLS

Operators are fully armed on missions. Each operator carries two pistols and an HK-416 rifle. They are also equipped with bullets, knives, grenades, and medical kits. Underneath, they wear **Kevlar** vests for protection.

Kevlar: a strong, bulletproof fiber

DELTA
FORCE

Kevlar vest
M9 Beretta pistol
HK-416 rifle

Operators wear **disguises** instead of uniforms. For daytime missions, operators dress like local people. In Afghanistan, some grew long beards and wore traditional clothing.

Most Delta Force missions are carried out at night. Operators wear night-vision goggles to see their enemies in the dark. They wear black clothing so enemies can't see them.

disguise: a costume that hides who a person is

On a mission in Bosnia, an operator wore a gorilla costume to surprise the enemy.

SECRET SUCCESSES

Delta Force is a secret team of skilled, smart soldiers. They catch terrorists. They rescue hostages. They sneak through foreign countries to gather information. These soldiers use speed, surprise, and strength to keep the United States safe.

GLOSSARY

CIA (SEE EYE AY)—a U.S. government organization that gathers secret information from other countries; CIA stands for Central Intelligence Agency

disguise (dis-GYZ)—a costume that hides a person's appearance

hijack (HYE-jak)—to take illegal control of a vehicle

hostage (HOSS-tij)—a person held prisoner by an enemy

Kevlar (KEV-lar)—a strong, bulletproof fiber used in equipment that protects soldiers

operator (OP-uh-ray-tur)—a soldier who is a member of Delta Force

selection (suh-LEK-shunhn)—the testing period where soldiers are picked for Delta Force

terrorist (TER-ur-ist)—someone who uses violence to achieve a goal

READ MORE

Alvarez, Carlos. *Army Delta Force.* Armed Forces. Minneapolis: Bellwether Media, 2010.

Besel, Jennifer M. *The Army Rangers.* Elite Military Forces. Mankato, Minn.: Capstone Press, 2011.

Riley, Gail Blasser. *Delta Force in Action.* Special Ops. New York: Bearport Pub., 2008.

INTERNET SITES

FactHound offers a safe, fun way to find Internet sites related to this book. All of the sites on FactHound have been researched by our staff.

Here's all you do:

Visit *www.facthound.com*

Type in this code: 9781429653824

Check out projects, games and lots more at
www.capstonekids.com

INDEX